SPRING & SU~~MMER~~
CUSTOM~~S~~
IN SUSSEX, KENT & SURREY

By Fran & Geoff Doel and Tony Deane

This book is dedicated to the memories of
Peter Cole of Reigate
Sidney Doel of Hove
and Carol Watts of Edenbridge

MERESBOROUGH BOOKS
1995

Published by Meresborough Books, 17 Station Road, Rainham, Kent. ME8 7RS.
Meresborough Books is a specialist publisher of books on Kent and also of the monthly magazine 'Bygone Kent'. A full list of publications will be sent on request.

Also available:
'Mumming, Howling and Hoodening: Midwinter Rituals in Sussex, Kent & Surrey by Geoff & Fran Doel. A companion volume to this book. £3.50 (£4.00 by post).

ISBN 0948193832

Printed by Staples Printers Ltd, Rochester, Kent.

CONTENTS

Front cover: Shrovetide Street Football in Dorking c1897. A painting of Taffer Boult's band based on a photograph.   (Dorking Museum)

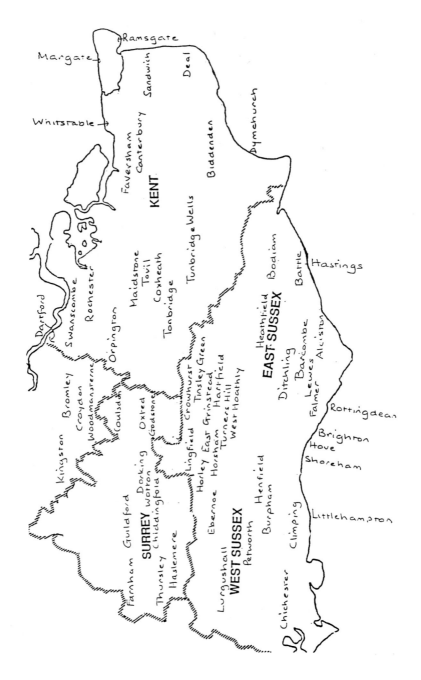

Map of Kent, Sussex and Surrey showing sites in the text.

PREFACE

This is the second in a projected three-book series sponsored by South East Arts and we are grateful to Judith Clark for her continued interest and encouragement. The first volume (published in December 1992) was entitled *Mumming, Howling and Hoodening – Midwinter Rituals in Sussex, Kent & Surrey* and South East Arts have also kindly offered support for a third volume on 'Legends'. One important group of customs in the three counties which have not fitted into either the Midwinter or Summer remits is of course the bonfire customs, which it is hoped to cover in a separate volume at some stage, along with other Autumn customs.

We should like to thank readers of the first volume for their enthusiastic response and encouragement and for additional information passed to us on Mummers Plays (particularly Carl Willetts for details of the Milton Regis Play), Blessing the Plough ceremonies and on the identification of one of the Hooden Horse photos (by Ron Shuttleworth) – all of which we hope to include in future editions/books.

One or two of our colleagues in the English Folk Dance & Song Society and Folk-lore Society, whilst welcoming the original research and the useful drawing together of relatively inaccessible material in the first volume, have expressed disquiet at our suggestions that elements of some seasonal customs are ancient and possibly religious in origin. Some folklorists still seem to be suffering from a Marxist orientation which shies away from antiquity, religion, ritual and any 'contamination' from contact with the upper classes and their culture. The anthropological ideas of Frazer, the archetypal ideas of Jung, the erudite research of E.K. Chambers on the ritual origins of drama in Europe and even the ideas of the founder of EFDSS, Cecil Sharp, and his disciples the Kennedy family, based on extensive fieldwork, are too casually dismissed by those who perhaps lack their wide cultural knowledge. Fortunately in the broader academic world in Britain and America this is not the case and the religious impulse underlying folk drama and ritual analysed by Chambers is accepted as fundamental.

However, there is no doubt that folklorists went 'over the top' in the twenties and thirties in searching for Frazerian connections in world-wide rituals, and their successors are wise to exercise caution and separate fact from speculation. There are many fascinating folk customs documented in this volume which are neither ancient nor religious. But to anyone with any knowledge of mediaeval society or of human religious and social needs, the antiquity of the ritual pattern and the essentially religious impulse (often surviving as the need for good luck) underlying many of our seasonal folk customs is surely evident and at least worthy of consideration?

The aim of this series is to draw together information about the traditional culture of Kent, Surrey and Sussex to give residents and exiles a sense of connection to their roots. Despite a nineteenth century adage that the true Sussex man divides the world into two parts – Kent and Sussex form one division, and all the rest is 'the Sheeres' – there nevertheless seems to be considerable affinity in the folklore of all three counties featured here. It is hoped the material may also be useful in education and in preserving and reviving these vital links with our collective past. We should be most grateful to receive corrections, comments and new material from readers.

Fran & Geoff Doel, Tonbridge and Tony Deane, Reigate
1995

Chapter 1
VALENTINE'S DAY
'The Birds' Wedding Day'

Traditionally the birds mate on Valentine's Day and this has associations with the beginning of Spring. Chaucer makes central use of the tradition in his poem *The Parliament of Fowls* (c1382):

'For this was on seynt Valentynes day,
Whan every foul cometh there to chese his make,
Of every kynde that men thynke may,'

In Sussex it was known as 'The Birds' Wedding Day' and is the setting for the song *Dame Durden* which is found in the famous Copper Family collection of folksongs as well as elsewhere in the South of England:

'Twas on the morn of Valentine when birds began to prate
Dame Durden and her maids and men they altogether meet'

One interesting Valentine's Day custom frequently recorded in Sussex is that of choosing the first person you meet of the opposite sex (other than your own family) on St Valentine's Day to be your Valentine for the coming year. This tradition is recorded in Pepys' Diary for Valentine's Day 1662:

'Valentine's day. I did this day purposely shun to be seen at Sir W. Battens – *because I would not have his daughter to be my Valentine, as she was the last year, there being no great friendship between us now as formerly. This morning in comes W. Bowyer, who was my wife's Valentine, she having (at which I made good sport to myself) held her hands all the morning, that she might not see the paynters that were at work in gilding my chimney-piece and pictures in my dining-room.'* This reference suggests that the woman is obliged to choose the first man she sees on Valentine's Day and hide from others until the right one comes along.

Originally gifts were sent to one's Valentine, then, in the eighteenth century, love messages. Valentine cards were an earlier invention than Christmas cards in the nineteenth century and have continued in popularity until today in our three counties, but Valentine gifts are making a comeback.

Shrovetide Street Football in Dorking, c1897. (Dorking Museum)

'The Last Football Day in Dorking Streets', c1897 – Taffer Boult's Band. (Dorking Museum)

Chapter 2
SHROVETIDE
Pancakes and Football

Shrovetide derives from two Anglo-Saxon words meaning 'the time to be shriven' – ie to confess one's sins before (in pre-Reformation Britain) the 40 day Lenten fast in which the eating of meat, milk, eggs, butter and cheese were generally forbidden. This penitential season began on Ash Wednesday and on the day before, Shrove Tuesday, people were summoned to church by the 'shriving bell' to be shriven and spent the rest of the day in violent sports and feasting on the foods forbidden in the ensuing Lent made into pancakes. Pancakes survived the Reformation and are still traditional fare in many homes on Shrove Tuesday. In Maidstone, Kent, as in many other places, a 'pancake bell' was formerly sounded to replace the shriving bell after the Reformation.

Taylor's *Jack-a-Lent* (written 1630) includes a recipe for 'Seventeenth Century Pancakes':

'There is a thing called wheaten flowre, which the cookes doe mingle with water, eggs, spice and other tragicall, magicall inchantments, and they put it by little into a frying pan of boyling suet where it makes a confused dismall hissing (like the Learnean snakes in the reeds of Acheron, Stix, or Phlegeton), untill, at last by the skill of the Cooke, it is transformed into the forme of a Flap-jack, cal'd a pancake, which ominous incantation the ignorant people doe devoure very greedily.'

The famous Pancake Race at Olney in Buckinghamshire has been copied in the South-East in recent years at Bodiam and Tunbridge Wells. Shrove Tuesday was also traditionally a day in which the male element in the community came together to play a ball game before the austerity of Lent. Football was a favourite, particularly in the Surrey market town of Dorking.

'That was a good thing...they finished with that. They never did anybody any good. There was always a lot of trouble, broken windows and that sort of thing. There was nothing...for the boys watching to be proud of at all. A proper game of football's good but not like that. In the end they saw sense and stopped it.'

These are the words of Nancy Shepherd, 92 years old when she was recorded by her nephew, Tony Gowan, in 1984. Most of Dorking's citizens at the turn of the century did not share her opinions, but her father owned a small furniture-shop, which had to be boarded up every Shrove Tuesday to avoid broken windows, and so her comments confirm Surrey historian Matthew Alexander's view that Dorking's annual football match was finally banned at the behest of local tradesmen.

Alexander argued in a paper delivered during the same year as Nancy's recording that as the status of shopkeepers shifted from working to middle-class so they worried

John Sanford, Dorking Town Crier, who started the Dorking football game from 1860-1895.

(Dorking Museum)

more about their property, then became local councillors, even Members of Parliament. Instead of taking part in the football, they saw it as a threat and ultimately voted to ban it: a classic example of poacher turned gamekeeper.

Street football – usually, but not always, held on Shrove Tuesday – still survives as a traditional game in parts of England (for example Ashbourne in the Peak District, Sedgefield in Durham, Atherstone in Warwickshire, Workington and Alnwick – where it has been moved out of the town onto a field). In Scotland, too, the Jethart Ba' is kicked around Jedburgh in the Borders region. In Surrey, though, the game is extinct: once it shattered the peace of Epsom, Kingston, Richmond and, finally, Dorking, where it virtually died on police orders in 1897, struggling on in reduced circumstances until about 1905.

Many curious legends cluster around the origins of these football games. Kingston's game was said to commemorate the town's heroic resistance to a Danish invasion-force; the Danes were beaten, their leader decapitated and his head kicked around the town. Similar stories of decapitation exist in Jedburgh and in Kirkwall in Orkney, while in Atherstone, King John is said to have seen the game start. Matthew Alexander suggests that the Dorking game did not predate 1830, but other reports refute this and, certainly the game must have gained instant popularity if he is correct. Other Shrovetide games definitely originated much earlier: the first reference to Hurling, the Cornish version, was printed in 1584.

On Shrove Tuesday morning the people of Dorking witnessed a strange procession. The leading-man carried a wooden frame with three footballs suspended from it. On the frame's crossbar was written 'Wind and Water is Dorking's Glory', perhaps explained by the wind used to inflate the balls and the 'duckings' to be suffered by players in the forthcoming game or, more simply, by the appalling weather that often accompanied or followed the game. In 1878 the phrase was expanded into a rhyme by the addition of the first line: 'Kick Away, Both Whig and Tory'. After the frame-carrier came Taffer Boult's Band, named after a long-dead player. Until 1895 the band was led by Phil Stedman, still a local name, who carried a collecting-box allegedly to gather money for repairs to property, but more probably to satisfy the group's thirst. He was followed by five or six musicians, all male and clad in fancy dress, their faces daubed with soot and red-ochre. There were whistle-players, a triangle-rapper, a drummer and sometimes a fiddler, playing 'a peculiar air', now sadly forgotten. One character always dressed as a woman, acting the fool and exchanging banter with the crowd. An illustration of the group in the Dorking Museum suggests a close relationship with mumming and guising traditions, although the minstrel shows, so popular in the 1890s, could have exerted a major costume influence.

Prior to 1860 the 'Pancake Bell' rang out from Dorking parish church between 11am and noon to signal the womenfolk to cook the pancakes which would sustain their partners through the ensuing sport. Then shops were closed and shuttered and street-lamps covered with sackcloth; both children and adults enjoyed a half-day's holiday. At 2pm by the church clock the first ball was kicked off from the top of Church Passage by a local dignitary: from 1860 until his death in 1895 this honour was held by John Sanford, the Town Crier. This first ball, the 'Boys' Ball', was fought over solely by youngsters.

The game proper, with the 'Men's Ball', started at 3pm, when the mayhem also began in earnest. There were few rules: any number could take part; teams were drawn from the east and west ends of the town, Church Passage forming the boundary; and the Westerners usually won as that part of the town was the more populous. The East won in 1866, though, when they were augmented by a gang of railway navvies. The object of the game was to bring the ball to one of the teams' own goals, usually marked by a stream on the edge of the town. The ball, unlike the players' shins, was rarely kicked during the game, more often being carried, or 'hugged', occasionally into a pub where drinks were taken before restarting the game by throwing the ball from an upstairs window. Before the 1870s blood from the abbatoir in West Street was allowed to flow into the road and, when the ball landed in it, the players become smothered. This unfortunate practice died out at the same time as regular immersions in the Pippbrook stream, following several deaths from pneumonia.

At 5pm a third ball entered the fray, this one gilded. By 6pm the game finished whether or not the ball had reached a goal; if not the accolade was awarded to the side in whose territory the ball ended up. Hostilities then ceased and feuds were forgotton for another year as pubs filled to capacity with hundreds of players and up to two thousand spectators. Senior players and the Band took dinner, probably more liquid than solid, at the Sun Inn – Nancy Shepherd recalls it as 'the Gun' but both are now defunct – while, in the 1890s, the Church of England Temperance Society held a tea party.

Street Football in Dorking differed little from that played elsewhere and it ended in similar fashion to many other places. In Kingston, despite the mayor's dictum in 1857 that 'this is a free England and people should be allowed to do as they like', the game was banned nine years later following riots in the streets. It is perhaps worth mentioning that the mayor was a publican with a vested interest in thirsty footballers. The first move to call time in Dorking was made in the 1850s but the game survived until 1897 when a large police presence dispersed the crowd. It was in 1897 that a Football Defence Association fund was set up, including a generous donation from Mr Henry Attlee, a local magistrate and father of the future Prime Minister. All to no avail, for thereafter sporadic efforts to rekindle interest were dashed by arrests and fines. The last reports appeared in 1905 when several small boys had their names taken and their footballs confiscated.

Other violent Shrovetide sports included cockfighting (well documented at Petworth in Sussex) and cock throwing, where lead-weighted sticks (known as libbets) – also used to knock down fruit from trees – were thrown at a tethered cock to try to knock it out.

Brand's *Popular Antiquities* gives an amazing reason for this tradition (a similar tale is told about the origin of the custom of Hunting the Wren in Ireland):

'The old custom of throwing at cocks on Shrove Tuesday is said to date from the fact of the crowing of a cock having prevented our Saxon ancestors from

massacreing their conquerors, another part of our ancestors, the Danes, on the morning of a Shrove Tuesday, when they were asleep in their beds.'

The Sussex folklorist Tony Wales has drawn attention to the popularity of cock throwing at Billingshurst in the late eighteenth century and how a unitarian minister there helped its demise by pinning a poem *The Cock's Remonstrance on Shrove Tuesday* to his church door. The *Lewes Journal* of 1778 proclaimed:

'It is with great pleasure we can inform the public that the barbarous practice of throwing at cocks is now so universally exploded in these parts that Shrove Tuesday did not produce a single instance of those acts of riot and cruelty by which this day was long and shamefully characterised, in open defiance of humanity and all civil authority.'

Shrovetide was also noted for the making of effigies, particularly that of 'Jack o' Lent'. In 1646 the poet Quarles wrote in *The Shepherd's Oracle*:

'How like a Jack o' Lent
He stands, for boys to spend their Shrovetide throws
Or like a Puppit made to frighten crows'.

Shying stones or other missiles at a figure made to resemble an unpopular local person was a widespread practice throughout rural England during Lent until the mid nineteenth century. It continues, perhaps, at fairgrounds, in the form of Aunt Sallies.

Occasionally the puppet was replaced by a life-sized effigy, Judas Iscariot, perhaps, being the original target. In Haslemere the effigy was set up on a horse or donkey and paraded through the town. It was led from house to house while boys collected money, shouting: 'Jack's up! hurrah! hurrah!' A placard, placed around the figure's neck, detailed its alleged misdemeanours. The procession started from Shepherd's Hill and always visited the victim's house, until, at the end of the day, the effigy was burned or hanged. The practice was very similar to the more common Rough Music, or Skimmington Ride. Incidentally, a pub on Reigate Heath is called 'The Skimmington Castle'.

If no particular resident attracted villification a newcomer to the district might be 'welcomed' or an elderly inhabitant 'honoured'. One harmless old man, chosen simply for his age, shamed his persecutors. He walked around his gibbeted effigy, examined it very carefully and said: 'Good, very good, and here's half-a-crown for you' to the sheepish onlookers. 'Like whipped curs,' wrote Eric Parker in 1947, 'they slunk away.'

The unpleasant custom of Jack o' Lent died in Haslemere in 1852 with the appointment of the town's first policeman. The constable 'arrested' Jack, although a few days later, when over a hundred navvies marched through the streets with another effigy, no action was taken.

A correspondent to *The Gentleman's Magazine* reported seeing a strange custom in an unnamed East Kent village on the Tuesday before Shrove Tuesday in 1779:

'I found an odd sort of sport going forward: the girls, from 18 to 5 or 6 years old, were assembled in a crowd, and burning an uncouth effigy, which they called an Holly-Boy, and which it seems they had stolen from the boys, who, in another part of the village, were assembled together, and burning what they called an Ivy-Girl, which they had stolen from the girls; all this ceremony was accompanied with loud huzzah, noise and acclamations. What it all means I cannot tell, although I inquired of several of the oldest people in the place, who could only answer that it had always been a sport at this season of the year.'

Until the late nineteenth century a wake fair was held in Lent beneath the great yew-tree which still stands in Crowhurst churchyard in Surrey. Heavy drinking was the order of the day and each fairgoer would return home with a piece of yew-bark 'for luck'.

The Fourth Sunday in Lent was 'Pudding Pie Sunday' in Oxted, Surrey, when all the wives spent the day baking.

Chapter 3
EASTER AND SPRING
Buns, Marbles and Doles

The Venerable Bede, writing in the eighth century, tells us that 'Easter' is named from a pagan goddess Eostre, goddess of the dawn and the spring (cf the word 'east'). Earlier cultures presumably had Springtime festivals with special food, perhaps including eggs and specially baked bread, but much of our Easter folklore and celebrations today are of course overtly Christian or connected with sports which developed because of the time off work.

In Sussex the belief is that Spring starts at Heffle (Heathfield) Cuckoo Fair on April 14th, when an old woman lets a cuckoo out of a bag as celebrated in Kipling's poem *Heffle Cuckoo Fair*. Charlotte Latham refers to a more general belief in West Sussex that: *'a certain old woman of irascible temper has charge of all the cuckoos, and that in the spring she fills her apron with them, and if she is in a good humour allows several to take flight, but only permits one or two to escape if anything has happened to sour her temper.'*

Hot Cross Buns
Frederick Sawyer in his 1883 article on Sussex customs recorded some interesting traditions concerning Hot Cross Buns. Buns were frequently kept from one year to the next (he refers to a Brighton undertaker doing this) and sometimes hung up in cottages as preservation against fire and for use pounded in water as medicine. Some Sussex fishermen carried buns for protection against drowning and another belief was that bread or buns baked on Good Friday could never go mouldy.

Marble Playing
Marble playing was very popular in the last century and up until the First World War in our three counties during Lent and culminating on Good Friday. The nineteenth century antiquarian Rev. Parish comments:

'In the country districts in Sussex the marble season is strictly defined between Ash Wednesday and Good Friday, and on the last day of the season it seems to be the object of every man and boy to play marbles as much as possible. They will play in the road at the church gate till the last moment before service, and begin again the instant they are out of church. Persons play at marbles on Good Friday who would never think of playing on any other day. Is it possible that it was appointed a Lenten sport, to keep people from more boisterous and mischievous enjoyments?'

This is a very plausible suggestion, especially as 'boisterous and mischievous enjoyments' frame the austere Lenten period on Shrove Tuesday and Easter Monday

Marbles Championship at the Greyhound public house, Tinsley Green, West Sussex.
(Tony Deane)

in many parts of the country. Frederick Sawyer was told by James Rolf, 'an old Brighton fisherman', that Brighton fishermen used to commence playing marbles on Ash Wednesday and continue through Lent to Good Friday. (Mr Sawyer records this in 1883 and also mentions Cuckfield as a particularly keen area for the game.)

A whole technical vocabulary for playing marbles exists in Sussex dialect; some of the terms have taken on a wider currency, for example 'inching', defined by the *Dictionary of Sussex Dialect* as:

'The practice of the privilege a shooter at marbles has of approaching with his hands the target so that the shot is less in length: sometimes only a span.'

Nowadays competitive marble playing survives only in pockets: at Battle in East Sussex (where the tolley or shooting marble is known as a 'bosser') and, more notably, in the area around Gatwick Airport. There are marble-rinks outside pubs in Charlwood, Turner's Hill and a few other nearby villages, but the centre of the marble-playing world is Tinsley Green in West Sussex. There the chink of the old game vies with the roar of aircraft from Gatwick every Good Friday.

The Greyhound Inn, Tinsley Green, has hosted the British and World Marbles Championship on Good Friday since 1932, when the event was founded by an enthusiast from nearby Horley. Among the early champions was the folksinger George 'Pop' Maynard, whose family team won the cup several times in the 1940s. Another great player, Sam Spooner, is commemorated by a plaque outside the pub; he took part in the 1932 championship using the same shooting marble, or 'tolley', that he had used as a player in the 1880s. Modern teams often carry graphic names like the 'Tinsley Tigers', the 'Handcross Rebels', the 'Moonshiners', the 'Turner's Hill Tolleymen', the 'Bakewell Tarts' – a ladies team – and the 'Black Dog Boozers' and the 'Barrel Scrapers', champions in 1994 and 1995 respectively. The game is popular in parts of the United States and American teams have won the World Title several times: in 1975 American visitors beat the previously-invincible 'Toucan Terribles', named in an attempt to gain sponsorship from Guinness.

Championship marbles, 'Ring Taw', is a more complex game than the schoolboy version and might be compared to outdoor snooker. It has been suggested that it was originally played in church porches by men waiting for the Good Friday service to begin. A circle of forty-nine marbles is set down in the middle of a sanded ring, six feet in diameter. Teams of six, each with his or her own tolley, try to knock these marbles from the ring; the tolleys are flicked by the thumb from a crooked index-finger. Pushing, or 'fudging', is against the rules, which are strictly applied by a referee. The first team to dislodge 25 marbles is the winner.

An imaginative story of the Tinsley Green game's origins (so far only traceable back 30 years) is that, during the reign of Elizabeth I, a Tinsley Green girl was courted by two suitors, one from Surrey, the other from Sussex. To win her hand, they played a series of contests: archery, falconry and wrestling. When no clear winner emerged they decided upon a game of marbles. Unfortunately, the tale ends there and the maiden's fate remains a mystery – but marbles has been played at Tinsley Green ever since. Despite attempts to commercialise the game in recent years, particularly by Capital Radio in the 1980s, marbles has fiercely maintained its bucolic spirit.

Good Friday skipping at Brighton, c1937-9.   (R. Merrifield)

The Rev. Parish records another variant of the Sussex game of marbles known as 'Bigoring':

'A marbles game where the players contribute equally to the pool of marbles placed in the middle of a ring 3 feet or so in diameter, and shoot in turns from the circumference. If the player knock out one or more marbles they are his spoil, and he can go on so long as he remains in the ring and gets one or more marbles out at each shot. If he remain in and fail to get a marble out he becomes dead and can be shot at by the others.' This is also known as 'Shoot Through the Ring'.

Good Friday Skipping

In Brighton, as in many other coastal communities, the fishermen did not go out to sea on Good Friday out of respect for Christ. Instead they organised skipping, using their long and thick fishing ropes. In Brighton, Good Friday was sometimes called 'Long Rope Day'.

The Rev. Parish records the nineteenth century custom:

'On Good Friday it is the custom of the Brighton fishermen to skip in the fish market. A rope is swung by two men and all and sundry are expected to run in and skip. Formerly every street had its own long rope. The practice is said to have a religious origin, the rope representing the one with which Judas hanged himself. The Priory of St Bartholomew is known to have encouraged it.'

A correspondent to *Notes and Queries* mentioning 1863 says that:

18

'In Brighton on this day the children in the back streets bring up ropes from the beach. One stands on the pavement on one side, and one on the other, while one skips in the middle of the street. Sometimes a pair (a boy and a girl) skip together, and sometimes a great fat bathing-woman will take her place, and skip as merrily as the grandsire danced in Goldsmith's "Traveller". They call the day "Long Rope Day".' (Long Line Day is another name.)

Frederick Sawyer records 'scores of skippers' on the Level at Brighton on Good Friday 1883. Olive Doel remembers Good Friday skipping in the 1920s in Brighton:

'As a girl my parents ran the Queensbury Arms (also known locally as 'The Hole in the Wall') just off Brighton seafront. On Good Friday morning I used to cross over to the fishermen's market or hard between the piers and join in the skipping. The fishermen twirled two long ropes in different directions and we used to try to jump over one without being hit by the other. The ropes were very heavy and could give you a nasty whack.'

The custom stopped at Brighton at the beginning of the Second World War, when Brighton seafront was fortified, but moved for a number of years to the Rose Cottage Inn at Alciston, where it survived until the 1960s. Much earlier, in the 1850s, there are records of skipping on a tumulus in what is now Palmeira Square, Hove, on Good Friday. This tumulus, in which was found the famous Amber cup, was levelled by the Corporation.

Good Friday long rope skipping was recently discreetly revived at Brighton by Andrew Duncan, whose grandmother was involved in it between the wars. Other less-researched sponsored inland revivals have lost all contact with fishermen, tradition and local communities and have turned this distinctive custom into a mass-produced showpiece.

Doles, Alms and Maunds

Perhaps because of the significance of the Last Supper and the Maundy traditions (based on Christ's command to his disciples to assist the poor), Easter was a favourite time for bequests giving annual doles to the poor. The most interesting one in our region is the Chulkhurst charity of the wool town of Biddenden in Kent.

Elisa and Mary Chulkhurst are legendary Siamese twins said to have been born in 1100 and died in 1134. The charity was endowed by rents from about twenty acres of land and a smallholding known as 'the Bread and Cheese Lands' (and possibly also originally from produce). The property has recently been sold for housing development (Chulkhurst Avenue etc) and the money invested to maintain the charity along with rents from the Old Workhouse and a small plot of land. An area of the former Bread and Cheese Lands has also been made into a children's playground.

We have records of the dole in 1646 and 1656 when the Puritan Minister, William Horner, tried unsuccessfully to claim the Bread and Cheese Lands as part of the Glebe lands. The case reached 'His Highness' Court of Exchequer' in 1656 and the judgement given was that the lands bequeathed belonged to the parish. The original charity was cheese, bread and beer given to widows of the parish in the church on Easter Sunday. In 1682 the Rev. Giles Hinton complained to Archbishop

The Biddenden Dole,1902   (Sir Benjamin Stone)

Sancroft that the custom: *'even to this time is with much disorder and indecency observed and needs a regulation by His Grace's Authority'*. It was moved to the church porch.

The Victorians changed the venue to the workhouse, the day to Easter Monday and the beverage from beer to a packet of tea. In 1872, 538 loaves were distributed. The charity was consolidated with three other small local charities in 1907. Nowadays all widows and senior citizens of the parish can receive the dole between 10 and 11am on Easter Monday from the old workhouse (now called 'The White House') at the west end of the village on Sissinghurst Road and money at Christmas. Tourists are given a hard inedible biscuit made from flour and water with a traditional pattern stamped on it of two women whose bodies seem to be joined. Over their heads are their names and the skirt of one figure has 'in 1100' inscribed on it and the other the number '34'.

According to Edward Hasted the Kent Historian, in 1792, the figures had only appeared on the biscuits about 50 years earlier and had originally been intended to represent the widows benefiting from the dole rather than the sisters. He suggested that the dole had been more recently (he was unable to establish the date) endowed by a pair of unjoined maiden ladies called Preston. In Hasted's day the biscuits seem to have been unnamed and undated.

The story of the Chulkhurst twins first appears in an eighteenth century locally printed broadside, which describes the death of one sister and the refusal of the survivor to be separated (*'as we came together we will go together'*) and her consequent

A Biddenden Biscuit, 1902.   Biddenden Village Sign.   (Geoff Doel)
(Sir Benjamin Stone)

death six hours later. A poem found in the old charity documents sounds eighteenth or nineteenth century.

'The moon on the east oriel shone
Through slender shafts of shapely stone
The silver light so pale and faint,
Shewed the twin sisters and many a saint
Whose images on the glass were dyed:
Mysterious maidens side by side
The moonbeam kissed the holy pane
And threw on the pavement a mystic stain.'

In 1569 Thomas Taylor of Cranbrook bequeathed about seven acres of woodland, now called Poors Wood, for the use of the poor. Timber from Poors Wood was used to build the workhouse from where the Chulkhurst Charity is now distributed. This bequest was administered alongside the Chulkhurst Charity by the Parish and is said to have 'brought in a good return in timber sales from time to time'.

The Kelly Bequest

Dorothy Tutt has sent us details of another dole – the Kelly bequest – which takes place on the first Sunday in July (originally 21st December until St Thomas's Day was moved by the Church of England to July 3rd) at St Leonard's Church, Chelsham in Surrey. Thomas Kelly (1772-1855) a local lad who became Lord Mayor of London,

Biddenden Dole, 1984 (Geoff Doel)

never forgot his humble origins and his will benefited the village with a £600 bequest. Dorothy Tutt in her excellently researched article on Thomas Kelly for *Local History Records* writes:

'One third was to provide a gift of bread, a quartern loaf for an adult and a two pound loaf for a child. This "shall be distributed on St Thomas's Day yearly, after a Service in the Parish Church, by the Incumbent or Curate and Churchwardens and at their discretion amongst the most deserving of the poor, after the preaching of the sermon".

...In 1898, 263 parishioners from 54 households claimed bread, of these 111 were children. Tea was sometimes given, as in 1912 when 53 people received three quarters of a pound each. For about sixty years now, tickets or vouchers have been given, to be exchanged at a local shop for bread or the equivalent in flour.'

A Founder's Day celebration takes place in Croydon Parish Church on March 22nd each year. Archbishop Whitgift laid the foundation stone for Croydon alms-houses on that date in 1618 and the annual ceremony, when a wreath is placed on his tomb, is now attended by occupants of the almshouses plus masters and boys from Whitgift School.

Dicing for the Maid's Money

In 1674 an abstemious Guildford philanthropist, John How, left £400 to be invested for the benefit of local maidservants and nannies. The dispensation of the annual interest – about £12 – produces an odd ceremony held on the first Thursday in March each year in Guildford Guildhall. Then two suitable candidates, neither of whom should live in an alehouse, throw dice, the highest score deciding the winner. Originally no second prize was awarded but now a legacy of £600 left by one John Parsons for apprentice-boys has been co-opted for this role. Thus, the interest on £600 being greater than that on £400, the winner becomes the loser. Today the main problem with the Maid's Money custom is finding suitable applicants.

Easter Sunday – the Dancing Sun
As in many parts of Britain, there was a belief in Sussex that the sun dances on Easter Sunday to celebrate Christ's resurrection. Rev. Parish records that:
'There is a tradition that the sun dances on the morning of Holy-Sunday, but nobody has ever seen it because the devil is so cunning that he always puts a hill in the way to hide it.'

Easter Monday – Egg Rolling
On Easter Monday egg rolling is practised in the Calverley Grounds in Tunbridge Wells. This is a recent innovation, but it is a traditional practice in some other parts of Britain.

Lady Day
March 25th celebrates the Annunciation – ie the revelation of Gabriel to the Virgin Mary. In the twelfth century it was regarded as the beginning of the year and remained important legally as a quarter day, along with Michaelmas (29th Sept) when rents and bills were paid and hiring fairs held for farm labourers to contract themselves.

The diarist John Evelyn, of Wotton House, near Dorking, under a dairy reference to March 25th 1672, describes a journey from Margate to Rochester:
'through a country the best cultivated of any that in my life I had anywhere seen, every field lying as even as a bowling-green, and the fences, plantations, and husbandry, in such admirable order, as infinitely delighted me...Observing almost every tall tree to have a weathercock on the top bough, and some trees half a dozen, I learned that, on a certain holiday, the farmers feast their servants; at which solemnity, they set up these cocks, in a kind of triumph.'

Hocktide
Hocktide – the second Monday and Tuesday after Easter – is of obscure origin. Rev. Parish in his *Dictionary of Sussex Dialect* records without comment the extraordinary tradition that in Sussex Hock-Monday was *'kept as a festival in remembrance of the defeat of the Danes in King Etheldred's time'*. In Kingston pre-Reformation Hock Games are recorded, when women organised a street 'gaderynge' by capturing men with ropes and forcing them to contribute to church funds; the men retaliated, demanding kisses rather than money. Such sexual mock-conflict was typical of hocktide activities elsewhere in England.

Tyting Dancing

On April 14th 1868 *The County Chronicle and Weekly Advertiser* reported *'the usual gathering of the lower orders'* on Good Friday at Tyting Farm, near Guildford. The paper went on to describe fruit-vendors and itinerant musicians and to suggest that, for the sake of propriety and religious observance, the event should be moved to Easter Monday. Two years later *The Times* mentioned a 'pilgrimage' to St Martha's, the chapel-crowned hill above Tyting Farm.

The gathering took place on Bent Piece, an area of flat land at Tyting Farm. There was no charter so technically the event could not be described as a fair: *'a kind of rural fete'* was *The Surrey Advertiser*'s verdict in 1867. Matthew Alexander considers that it probably dated from the early nineteenth century, despite references to a custom *'lost in the obscurity of time'*, and it appears not to have outlived the century of its birth.

Tyting's attractions included hockey, shying orange-peel and 'kiss-in-the-ring' but the three thousand strong crowds' favourite pastime was massed dancing. This lasted until 8 or 9 o'clock at night, accompanied by musicians playing brass instruments, accordions and drums; in 1871 a blind fiddler and his wife joined the players. Like many other customs, now vaunted as 'time-honoured', the Tyting Dancing probably grew out of the oppressed working-man's need for a holiday: the picnics on the Devil's Jumps, near Thursley, for instance.

It seems that the beginning of the end for dancing at Tyting came in 1871 when an evangelistic preacher ranted against turning Good Friday into a party, 'giddy and gay'. He was pelted with orange-peel for his trouble. Today there is no sign of the jollifications at Tyting although it is possible that Halfpenny Lane, leading to the farm, recalls the admission charge.

Chapter Four
MAY DAY
May Garlands, Maypoles
and Jacks-in-the-Green

May customs frequently celebrate the arrival of Summer and the burgeoning of Nature. Until the end of the nineteenth century May 1st was an unofficial holiday and in the morning children used to carry May Garlands round, sometimes with a doll inside which was said to represent the Queen of May or the Virgin Mary. All over the south of England, the Midlands and East Anglia similar songs were sung, combining joyous seasonal elements, requests for customary tribute and reminders of man's mortality. Typical is this one from Whitstable in Kent which informs us that in addition to the garlands they carry the singers have visited the woods early on May morning in order to 'Bring in the May' in the form of boughs:

The Whitstable May Song
'The first of May is garland day, we wish you a merry May,
We hope you like our May garland because it is May day.
A branch of May we have brought you and at your door we stand,
It is but a sprought, but well budded out by the work of our poor hands.

This morning is the first of May, the primest of the year,
So people all both great and small, we wish you a joyful year.
We have been wandering all the night and almost all this day
And now returning back again, we've brought you in the May.

I have a purse upon my arm and drawn with a silken string.
It only wants a few more pence to line it well within.
Come give us a cup of your sweet cream, or a jug of your fine beer
And if we live to tarry the town, we'll call another year.

The life of man is but a span, he's cut down like the grass,
But here's to the green leaf of the tree, as long as life shall last.
So why not do as we have done the very first day of May?
And from our parents we have come, to roam the woods so gay.

And now we bid you all adieu and wish you all good cheer,
We'll call once more unto your house before another year.
God bless our Land with power and might, send peace by night and day.
God send us peace in England, and send us a joyful May.

This song is quoted by Don Minifie in an interesting article in *English Dance & Song* which describes the traditional Jack-in-the-Green festival at Whitstable, which

25

Whitstable Jack-in-the-Green and May Celebrations, 1912.

The controversial 'Killing' of the Jack-in-the-Green by Mad Jack's Morris, Hastings 1987.
(Geoff Doel)

on May Day led a procession of Morris Dancers from the Horsebridge outside The Duke of Cumberland to the site of the Maypole, the supposed end to the custom in 1912 with the burning to death of the Jack who was allegedly set fire to, and the custom's revival in the 1970s. Neither Don Minifie nor we have been able to trace an account of the accident in the press (the information in the article came orally from a Whitstable historian). Similar legendary undocumentable endings of customs through fatalities have entered the tradition all over England. The Jack-in-the-Green is traditionally a man in a wicker casing stuffed with evergreens and ignition whilst on parade resulting in death does seem unlikely. We should be grateful to hear of any further information about this story.

Gordon Newton and Keith Leech with Mad Jack's Morris have also made stimulating revivals at Rochester (the original remembered by Russell Thorndike from his boyhood days in the 1890s) and Hastings. The festivities now extend over three days in the early May holiday and include a great deal of energetic morris dancing. The Hastings Jack is slim-line and is associated with May garlands; a controversial aspect is the killing and resurrection of the Jack at the end of the festival as there is no documentary evidence (as far as we are aware) for the death of the Jack in the English tradition. We understand that Keith Leech has been influenced by accounts of customs in Germany and France. The Rochester Jack is chunkier and accompanied by groups of children dressed up as chimney sweeps who join the grand procession. Jacks-in-the-Green were associated with chimney sweeps in London in the nineteenth century and the sweeping fraternity seem responsible for taking the customs to towns in the south east such as Bromley, Orpington, Hastings (the Lee family), Brighton, Lewes, Henfield, Rochester, Ramsgate, Farnham, Kingston-upon-Thames and Horsham. Henry Burstow, a bellringer and folksinger with a repertoire of over 400 songs, recalled in his *Reminiscences of Horsham* (1911):

'May Day, or Garland Day, was a very jolly time for us youngsters, not only because it was a holiday, but also because we used to pick up what seemed to us quite a bit of money. Early in the morning we would get up our best nosegays and garlands, some mounted on poles and visit the private residents and tradespeople. We represented a well recognised institution, and invariably got well received and patronised...

'On this day, too, we had Jacks-in-the-Green. The chimney sweeps used to dress up in fancy costumes and in evergreens and flowers, and accompanied by a fiddler or two, parade and dance all round the town and neighbourhood. There were two sets of Jacks-in-the Green when I was a boy (c1850), the Potter and the Whiting parties, and considerable rivalry existed between them.'

Dorking had its Jack-in-the Green until at least the 1850s; surrounded by clean-faced sweeps in bright clothing he danced to the rattle of hoe and shovel. In Tadworth the Jack-in-the-Green custom lasted until the outbreak of the First World War, when children carrying posies of flowers would collect pennies from door-to-door. Generally, the custom began to die out after sweeps' boys were banned by law in 1864.

Rochester's Jack-in-the-Green, May 1989.
(Geoff Doel)

Jack-in-the-Green, Lambeth 1894.

(Tony Foxworthy)

In former Kent and Surrey environs close to London, Jacks-in-the-Green are recorded in Lambeth, Greenwich, Kennington and Lewisham, where a vivid eye-witness account by Frank Lewis in 1894 is cited in Roy Judge's invaluable book *The Jack in the Green:*

'May Day, 1894, at Lewisham. In the High Street, at the inn near St Mary's Church, we saw a Jack with a Queen of the May, two maidens-proper, one man dressed as a woman, and a man with a piano-organ. The organ was playing a quick tune and the Queen and the maidens danced round the Jack with a kind of "barn-dance" step, the Jack turning the other way. The man-woman sometimes danced with the maidens, turned wheels, and collected pence. The Jack was a bottle-shaped case covered with ivy leaves and surmounted by a crown of paper roses. The Queen wore a light-blue dress and had a crown similar to Jack's. The senior maiden wore a red skirt and a black body; the junior wore a white dress; each wore a wreath of roses. The man-woman wore a holland dress and over it a short sleeveless jacket; his face was blackened, and had a Zulu hat trimmed with red, the brim being turned up.'

Some authorities believe that Jacks-in-the-Green developed as a moving substitute for Maypoles which had been banned by act of Parliament in 1644, Some Maypoles re-appeared at the Restoration as a symbol of restored monarchy. On May Day 1660, four weeks before King Charles' return, Samuel Pepys was told *'how the people of Deale* (Deal in Kent) *have set up two or three Maypoles and have hung up their flags upon the top of them.'* Pepys also records his wife in the custom of 'Gathering May Dew' (good for the complexion) early in the morning – in a previous century Katherine of Aragon and her ladies in waiting had done this in the Greenwich area.

Other Maypoles were re-introduced as a part of the Victorian 'Merrie England' movement perhaps such as the Maypole remembered by Lucy Baldwin (wife of the Prime Minister) at Rottingdean in the 1880s:

'On the first of May I remember a Maypole and the children dancing round it on the village green. The pole had a bunch of flowers on the top and...streamers coming from it. The custom has now died out, but later the children would bring round small posies, sing their little song and then violently ring your front door bell. The song ran as follows:

"First of May, My birthday.

Give us all A 'oliday"

They were quite content with a couple of pennies, but other small parties would come round in such numbers that it called forth a protest from the village school-master, with a request that no money should be given before 12, when the children came out of school.'

At Petworth (Sussex) the children sang as they carried round their garlands:

'The first of May is Garland Day,

So please remember the garland,

We don't come here but once a year,

So please remember the Garland.'

Edwardian Maypole Dancing.   (Geoff and Fran Doel Collection)

Children with May Garlands, Horsham.   (Tony Wales Collection)

Thomas Trowsdale gives an interesting account of 'Garland Day' in Sevenoaks, Kent, in 1880:

'This morning I had the pleasure of witnessing a lingering remnant of the olden observances of "Merrie May-day". Numbers of children went about from house to house in the Sevenoaks district in groups, each provided with tasteful little constructions which they called May-boughs and garlands. The former were small branches of fruit and other early blossoming trees secured to the end of short sticks, and were carried perpendicularly. One of these was borne by each of the children. Two in every group carried between them, suspended from a stick, the "May-garland", formed of two transverse willow hoops, decorated with a profusion of primrose and other flowers, and fresh green foliage...At every door the children halted and sang their May-day carol, in expectation of a small pecuniary reward from the occupants of the house.

'...Middle-aged matrons who have resided in this part of the "garden of England" all their lives, speak in terms of pardonable pride of the immense garlands of their girlhood. Forty years ago, I am told, the May-garlands often exceeded a yard in diameter, and were constructed in a most elaborate manner.'

The Sussex folklorist Lilian Candlin recalls that her mother, born in 1870 in Lewes:

'went early to the Daisy Bank – a grassy slope opposite the old Fox Inn at Southeram, on the 1st of May to gather wild flowers...The flowers were made into a garland which she took around to the neighbours who gave her a penny or a cake for the sight of it.'

At Shoreham in Sussex festivities begin early in the morning with dancing and for many years it has been traditional to 'knock up' local dignitaries (ie hammer on their doors to rouse them) as a beginning to May morning.

Maypoles were erected in many Surrey towns and villages: even Croydon, where they survived into the 1850s. In Dorking youngsters paraded through the town on May morning, crying: *'Please, ma'am, remember the day, the first of May, when I come round with my maypole.'* They met at noon in South Street and sold their 'poles' for a penny each to Mr W. Norman, a grocer; the poles were, in fact, bunches of wild flowers and sometimes up to fifty bunches were displayed outside the grocer's shop. The children knew the custom as 'maypoling' and it was obviously a variant of garlanding.

In 1891 the rector of Ockley rued the demise of garlanding. As with maypoling, children circulated the village, selling garlands of flowers for a penny each. Each garland was made up of three or four hoops covered with leaves and flowers, then linked into a globe or wreath; by the end of the last century this complex structure had degenerated into a stick with a few flowers on the end of it.

Similar customs existed in Farnham, Kingston, Oxted and elsewhere in Surrey. The diarist John Aubrey reported that in Lingfield the garlands were made of Mid-summer Silver, 'an unknown herb', which Geoffrey Grigson translates as silverweed. In Hambledon the children chanted a rhyme:

'The first of May is Garland Day,
Give me a penny and I'll go away.'

Children with May Garlands, Cowfold 1910.　　　　　　　(Tony Wales Collection)

They collected pennies or, from more generous villages, buns and cakes. Another rhyme, from Weybridge, reflects May carols from all over England:

'A bunch of flowers I've brought you
And at your door I'll stand;
Its a lovely time and a lovely day
And we come from the Lord's right hand.'

Because children played truant from school to 'go garlanding' with the ending of the unofficial May Day bank holiday about 1880, some schools introduced their own May revels. John Ruskin is credited with inventing the idea of a May Queen, for a ceremony at Whitelands Teachers Training College, in 1888 (a famous painting survives of the pupil teachers dressed in white at the ceremony). Ruskin also helped to introduce ribbon-plaiting maypole dances from Europe to replace the traditional English garlanded maypoles. Dorking Girls' School added May Day sports to the curriculum in 1904, as the unofficial garlanding ceased at the Boys School.

The decking out of towns and villages with greenery appears to be an ancient tradition. Queen Elizabeth visited Sandwich in early May 1572, *'every house having a nombre of grene boughs standing against the dores and walls'*. May Day was known as 'Flowering Day' in the early nineteenth century, when Head Boys from Tonbridge School collected flowers from neighbouring gardens to decorate the town and classrooms. On the 2nd or 3rd May Masters and Wardens of the Skinners Company (which endowed Tonbridge Public School) visited for a procession and church service and the High Street was decorated with birch boughs. An account of 1799 mentions a dozen old women from the nearby almshouses strewing flowers at the doorway of the school for the governors to walk over. In 1825 the date for this visitation was moved to July.

Green boughs have an ancient significance in Kent. Tradition has it that the Man of Kent met William of Normandy near Swanscombe in 1067 each with a green bough in the left hand and a sword in the right, promising allegiance if he would maintain their ancient laws and privileges (such as gavelkind). Kentish bowmen fought at Agincourt under a banner showing an arm upraised with a sword rising from green boughs.

Many occupations would celebrate May Day with May Garlands. Shepherds sometimes garlanded their sheep in Sussex and Sawyer, writing of May Day 1883, says:

'This day is known in Sussex as Garland Day, and is a favourite day with the Brighton fishermen for commencing mackerel fishing. When the fishermen start on this day, they decorate the masts of their boats with "garlands", while at other times they used to accompany the sweeps in their celebration of the day.'

The *Brighton Custumal* elaborates a system of 'fares' and 'shares' for the mackerel season (mid April–mid June) and for other fishing; the catch or its value was divided between master of the ship, men, vicar and churchwardens and defence of the town from the French.

'The Play of Robin Hood' – 'very proper to be played in May-games', printed c1562. Revived in the 1980s and 1990s by the Tonbridge Mummers. In this scene Friar Tuck's dogs attack Robin's outlaws.
(Archie Turnbull)

The dance of Friar Tuck and Maid Marian from the same play.
(Fran Doel)

Chapter 5
THE MAY GAMES and
MORRIS DANCING

In many parts of Europe traditions survive of all male dances in costume at set seasonal times of the year with fixed steps; many of these traditions are hundreds of years old. In England, although the type of dance, numbers of dancers and time of year can vary from area to area, this form of dancing has been for five hundred years known under the generic title of Morris dancing.

Morris dancing was particularly associated with the May Games, which were usually held at Whitsun or even as late as June in England. Extensive records of the May Games are found in the Churchwarden's Account Book of Kingston-upon-Thames from 1503-1538 and have been analysed by June Sampson in *The Story of Kingston* and by David Wiles in *The Early Plays of Robin Hood*.

In 1393 William of Wykeham, Bishop of Winchester, issued a mandate stating that, as both clergy and laity used Kingston churchyard for ball-games, stone-throwing and other activities and had caused much damage, *'juggling, the performance of loose dances, ballad-singing, the exhibiting of shows and spectacles and the celebration of other games in the churchyard'* were to be banned on pain of excommunication.

The games were detailed in the sixteenth century Churchwardens' Accounts as including the 'Kyngham' (alternatively called the 'Church Ale') and the 'Robin Hood'; Morris dancers are mentioned in 1510 when six pairs of dancing shoes were purchased; in 1516 when they had a crown; in 1536 when they wore coats of fustian and bells on their garters; and in 1536 when their eight pairs of garters were for six dancers, the fool and the 'mowren' (possibly a maid-marian figure played by a man) clad in buckram. Collections of money – 'gaderynges' – were taken (at first by the May King and Queen and then by Robin Hood) and passed to the church-wardens to settle all expenses; any surplus was used for church maintenance or poor relief.

The May Games began with the church bells ringing at dawn above houses strewn with greenery. There was a gaily-coloured maypole – abolished during the Commonwealth but revived later – and a May Queen. Dancing round the revived maypole continued until the mid nineteenth century, when the pole was carried through the Market place and erected in the Apple Market.

The Robin Hood, at Whitsun, was performed by green-suited archers, led by a Robin Hood figure, giving archery displays; the performance also featured Maid Marian (whose part seems to have been taken by a male Morris dancer when the dancers got involved), Little John, Friar Tuck and a minstrel (Alan A'Dale?).

The play of 'Robin Hood and the Potter' performed by the Tonbridge Mummers at Anne of Cleves House, Lewes, June 1993.

(Geoff Doel)

The Kyngham was a Summer play featuring the King and Queen of May (sometimes interchangeable, at Kingston and elsewhere, with Robin and Marian) plus nine dancers and attendants. Kingston Museum houses a stained-glass window (a twentieth century reproduction of a seventeenth century design) depicting the Kyngham with its characters and costumes. The play sometimes travelled by boat to other Thameside towns such as Richmond and Walton.

The local dancers' costumes were owned by Kingston parish while, in Guildford, the parish of Holy Trinity hired out Morris gear. In Georgian times a Guildford shopkeeper sold Morris bells and, as late as 1869, the curate of Puttenham praised one of his flock as 'by far the best dancer in the whole neighbourhood'. Morrismen wearing streamers and coloured ribbons accompanied Kingston's Jack-in-the-Green until the late 1800s, with a musician playing pipe-and-tabor. George Sturt (Bourne) author of The Wheelwright's Shop, recalled similar proceedings in Farnham. Archie Fuller of South Godstone described to collectors Dick Richardson and Ken Stubbs an eight man Morris team (rather than the usual six) at Godstone on the Surrey–Kent border between the Wars. An eight dancer tradition is recorded at Lichfield and Abingdon. Was this Godstone side a revival based on a tradition imported or a relic of the original Surrey Morris?

In Kent, Morris dancers are recorded as greeting Charles II on his return from exile in 1660 (but they may not have been a local team). Alan Austen has drawn our attention to a quotation in Countryside Mood from an unidentified parson in 1672 saying that 'Maidstone was formerly a very prophane town, insomuch that (before

The Hartley Morris, 1990s.   (Phil Burkin)

1640) *I have seen morrice dancing, cudgel playing, stoolball, cricket, and many other sports, openly and publicly on the Lord's day.'*

The following early reference in the West Sussex Records Office for Morris dancers in Chichester occurs for New Year's Day 1618 and is deposition to a magistrate of Anthony Combes of Chichester, a glover:

'That either the first night or the second night after New Years Day last past in Ano Domini 1617 (ie 1618) and within the time libellated this deponent between the hours of eight and nine of the clock at night standing talking with the said Richard Knight libellated in the north street of the city of Chichester aforesaid right over against the dwellinghouse of Mr Anthony Smith, scrivener, or a very little below the same house, then and there being present and talking with them one John Cowdry a witness also in this cause sworn and examined the said Richard Knight and this deponent and the said John Cowdry looking upon Morris dancers or maskers the said Richard Knight said to this deponent in the presence and hearing of the said John Cowdry that we (meaning himselfe and this deponent) heard better sport the last night or the other night next before, meaning thereby that they heard the said William Marner and Agnes Wytcher libellated together behind the street door of the dwellinghouse of George Evans libellated situate within the parish of St Peters in the North Stret of the City of Chichester aforesaid...'

A Winter reference to Morris dancing is unusual and the reference to 'maskers' may indicate a Winter custom such as Mumming – perhaps associated with a dance.

Sadly no traditional dances survive from Kent, Sussex and Surrey (though it is known that the Surrey tradition included a solo jig) but all three counties have all featured strongly in the Cotswold-style Morris revivals inspired by the collecting and teaching of Cecil Sharp and Mary Neale. Sutton's East Surrey team was established in 1926; Stansted Morris in Kent originated in 1934 and 'metamorphosed' into Hartley Morris (which is still thriving) in 1952. In Sussex the Chanctonbury and Martlett sides were founded in the early 1950s. The dance was traditionally men only, but there are now excellent ladies teams (such as Invicta in West Kent) and mixed sides such as Tonbridge, as well as highly traditional men-only sides such as Mr Jorrocks (centred on Frittenden, mid-Kent) who specialise in developing the Oddington Cotswold tradition. Under the guidance of Matthew Alexander, the Pilgrim Morris Men have revived May Day celebrations with music and dancing in the streets of Guildford. Ditchling Morris and Mad Jack's Morris from the Hastings area are among other fine Sussex teams, while the embryo Buckland Shag team from Reigate demonstrate Surrey's determination to join the trend towards reviving the Morris.

Increasingly Morris dancing can now be seen all Summer, and sometimes in the Winter too. And styles from other parts of England are now taking root in our counties, for example the Kettlebridge and Copperfield Clog sides in Kent represent a North-Western processional style and Wrotham White Star in Kent do North-Eastern short sword or rapper dances.

Opposite: The Chanctonbury Morris Men at the Shepherd and Dog, Fulking, 1950s.
(Doc Rowe Collection)

Beating the Bounds, St Nicholas Parish, Rochester. Probably Edwardian period.

Beating the Bounds at Hastings, 1920s. (Tony Wales Collection)

Chapter 6
ROGATIONTIDE, WHITSUN and OAK APPLE DAY

Rogationtide – Beating of the Bounds

A number of seasonal folk customs are perambulatory, the most obvious being the Beating of the Bounds, a ceremony often connected with Rogationtide (which precedes Ascension Day), when the parish boundaries were walked and the younger generation symbolically beaten or bumped to aid their territorial memories. The early Christian church seems to have been influenced by earlier cultures in its instigation of Rogationtide (Roman culture for example honoured Terminus the god of Boundaries and Romans processed through the fields at the festival of Ambarvalia in May).

Beating of the Bounds was regarded with suspicion by some Puritans and early Protestants, but Elizabeth I re-affirmed permission for clergy, churchwardens and parishioners to process on Ascension Day to define parish boundaries and offer up prayers for fruitful crops. The ceremonies were organised through the church and the Diocese of Chichester described their purpose in 1637 as for: *'knowing and distinguishing the bounds of the parishes, and for obtaining God's blessing upon the fruites of the ground.'* We have nineteenth century accounts from Burpham, Littlehampton and Chiddingford and traditions survived until early this century at Rochester, Canterbury and Barcombe and at Hastings into the 1920s. There have been numerous revivals in the three counties in recent years, the most famous being at Chailey, which was known to have Beating of the Bounds in the seventeenth century.

A most interesting account of a Rogationtide Beating of the Bounds from Dartford in 1850 survives:

'Last Tuesday the "lower bounds", or "short bounds", as they are often called, probably from their being twice as long as the "upper" or "long" bounds of Dartford parish, were perambulated. The "Roman road" for a long distance was, of course, the bound mark so long as it could be adapted to that purpose. Humpings, immersions in the brooks, and the other customary practices on these occasions were duly observed. As the boundary marks were more destroyed in this division than in the one perambulated the preceding week, a much longer time was occupied in the work before lunch-time. Certainly all parties were gratified beyond measure when the Long Reach tavern hove in sight...After luncheon the majority of the perambulators fancying their task was done, miraculously disappeared till dinner-time. Mr Landall and half-a-dozen other gentlemen, with the school-boys, started upon the work, and followed the Creek banks till they arrived at the spot where a boat was to have awaited them to cross the water to the opposite shore – for here, as Mr

Dunkin shewed, great alterations had been made by the stream in its course since the days when the parishes were parcelled out. The old water-courses and old embankments were however clearly defined;...at the division of the water, however, there was no boat'...

'...the worthies gloomily trudged on more than two miles to a spot where the bottom appeared to be harder...Here Mr Landall and some others determined upon crossing, as a labourer offered to carry persons over the ford for a gratuity without wetting them. After much labour, and getting covered with tenacious mud, Mr Landall safely got, Friar Tuck fashion, upon the man's shoulders, but alas, after four or five steps, both tumbled down into the stream and were thoroughly soused, amidst the laughter of those on terra firma...The perambulators then tramped more than ten miles, all the way back and afterwards again crossed the Creek. At 8 o'clock, sadly jaded and muddy, shorn of banners and followers, the three gentle-men and the boy arrived at the primal bound mark, in Maiden-lane, from which they had started, and just contrived to bump the individual who had at the com-mencement of the perambulation received a similar favour, amidst the acclamations of a vast crowd.'

The Beating of the Bounds between Croydon and Purley was last performed in the mid nineteenth century. A refreshment-booth, with a dray of beer, was set up near Foxley Hatch Gate, while schoolchildren stood in and under the Psalm Oak to sing *The Old Hundredth*.

In Dorking the Beaters of the Bounds were accompanied by the local vicar and officers of the parish. At certain points they were 'bumped' to impress the exact boundary-line; they also waded through streams, climbed high banks and generally enjoyed a rollicking good time. The final 'leg' involved banners waving to the music of fife and drum, perhaps Taffer Boult's Band of Shrovetide Football fame. Like Croydon's, Dorking's ceremony faded during the nineteenth century.

Tony Wales in his *Sussex Customs, Curiosities & Country Lore,* draws attention to accounts of Beating of the Bounds at the Sussex villages of Burpham (1810) and Chiddingfold (1869). At Burpham the minister led the procession, which stopped for prayers, the making of a cross on the ground and refreshments; 23 gallons of ale and quantities of bread and cheese and cake were provided. The Chiddingfold Beating of the Bounds involved a walk of 40 miles and took two days to complete; only three people took part!

Whitsun – The Climping Dragon

The Climping Dragon festival was one of the strangest Whitsun events in the south-east. The village of Climping, near Littlehampton in Sussex, was quite remote until the early 1970s. Its pub, the Black Horse, then managed by an elderly couple and basic in the extreme, became home between 1964 and 1971 to an extraordinary spectacle. A group of folksong enthusiasts from the Kent/London borders, notably Dave Watts and Robin Gray, regularly camped on the beach at Climping during the Whitsun weekend. In 1964 they set up the Climping Dragon festival based very closely on the Obby Oss ceremony of Padstow, Cornwall.

The Climping Dragon, late 1960s. (Dave Watts)

The police closed the road to the Black Horse, allowing the colourful dragon, built on to a frame carried by one of the group, to approach the pub, accompanied by musicians playing accordions and fiddles. The tune written by fiddle-player Mike Hutchison, was based on a popular 'surfing' song of the time, with elements of the Padstow May Song played in reverse. Once at the pub the day was given to serious drinking and singing.

Despite being a total invention, the Climping festival was accepted as a 'revival' and notes were kept in the headquarters of the English Folk Dance and Song Society. The Dragon was even invited by the late Bill Rutter to attend the Sidmouth International Folk Festival, where it danced side-by-side with the Padstow Old Oss. Strangely, years after the festival folded, the organisers discovered that Climping is, in fact, in an area noted for its dragon legends.

Empire Day

On Empire Day, May 24th, Reigate schoolchildren would congregate in the Castle Grounds, waving flags and singing patriotic songs. In nearby Headley children carrying flags walked in pairs to the rectory garden; there they enjoyed music from a hurdy-gurdy surmounted by a live monkey.

The Climping Dragon Ceremony – the Band, late 1960s.   (Dave Watts)

Oak Apple Day

Oak Apple Day, 29th May, celebrates the restoration of the monarchy in 1660 (and the consequent revival of seasonal folk customs) as well as Charles II hiding in the oak at Boscobel to avoid capture (and certain death). In Sussex it was known as 'Nettle Day' and if schoolboys failed to proclaim themselves royalists by wearing a spray of oak leaves, they were liable to have their bare legs beaten with stinging nettles.

When George III reviewed the troops at Coxheath in Kent in 1778, many gentlemen of Kent wore cockades of twigs of oak in their hats. And when George III reviewed the volunteers at Mote Park, Maidstone, in 1799, he and many of the Cabinet wore sprigs of oak, the Queen and princes decorated themselves with oak boughs and the shopkeepers also decorated their premises with oak boughs.

Another name for the day was 'Shik-Shak Day', probably from a seventeenth century expression meaning 'shit-sack' applied to anti-monarchists and other non-conformists. In Dorking, Farnham and Warlingham those not wearing sprigs of oak or the actual apples (parasitic galls found on oak trees) on May 29th were liable to insult or even assault for showing disrespect to the monarchy. Dorking church tower was decorated with oak boughs (a practice which continues at St Neot in east Cornwall), while Oak Apple Fair was held on Thorpe green until the outbreak of the Second World War. A descendant of Woodreve Wootton, who allegedly hid Charles II in an oak tree, once lived in Dorking.

Sadly, hardly anyone in our three counties celebrates Oak Apple Day any longer or wears oak sprays.

Chapter Seven
MIDSUMMER
Sheepshearing, Midsummer's Eve
Practices and Horn Fairs

Blessing the Sea

Many Summer customs relate to agriculture or fishing, such as the Blessing of the Sea at Hastings, when, on the Wednesday before Ascension Day, the Rectors of All Saints' and St Clement's churches lead a procession at 7pm to hold a service on the lifeboat, with hymns including *Abide with Me* and *Eternal Father Strong to Save*, prayers and a formal Blessing of the Sea. Folkestone's Blessing of the Sea ceremony is in July and Whitstable's in August.

Sheepshearing Customs

Sheepshearing customs were of particular interest in the South Downs area of Sussex. An 1849 article 'South-Down Shepherds and Their Songs at Sheepshearing' by R.W. Blencowe in the Sussex Archaeological Collections tells us that:

'Solitary as the shepherd's life generally was, there was one month in the year...that of June – the sheepshearing month – when they met together in considerable numbers to shear the various flocks. Their work was hard; but there was much that was enjoyable in it, for it was a season of social merriment, which contrasted strongly with the usual solitary tenor of their lives. The shearing used to be performed by companies, consisting generally of above thirty men, and most of them formerly were shepherds. Each company received its distinctive name from some place within the sphere of its labours. One was called...the Brookside, another the Portslade Company; each of them had a captain and lieutenant placed over it...'

'As soon as the company was formed, all the men repaired to the cottage of the captain, where a feast, which was called the "White Ram" was provided for them, and on this occasion the whole plan of the campaign was discussed and arranged.

'They generally got to their place of shearing about seven, and having breakfasted, began their work. Once in the forenoon and twice in the afternoon, their custom was "to light up", as they termed it; they ceased to work for a few minutes, drank their beer, sharpened their shears, and set to work again: their dinner-hour was one, but this was not the great meal of the day, supper being the time of real enjoyment, and when this was over, they would remain for several hours in the house, smoking their pipes, and singing their sheepshearing songs, in which they were joined by the servants of the farm, and sometimes the master and mistress of the house would favour them with their presence.'

An account survives in *Sussex Notes and Queries* of resolutions adopted at a meeting of the 'Company of Sheep Shearers' at the Swan Inn, Falmer, Sussex, on Wednesday 21st May 1828:

'1st – That the Men must be at the place they are going to work at 7 o'clock in the morning, they shall then immediately go to breakfast and be in the Barn ready to go to work at 8. To be allowed cold meat, or meat pies for their breakfast and one quart of Ale each man.

2nd – That they shall light up twice in the forenoon and be allowed each time one pint of Ale a man.

3rd – That they have at dinner boiled Meat, Meat Puddings, or Pies, what small beer they like and ½ pint of Strong Beer each Man after Dinner.

4th – That they be allowed to light up twice in the afternoon, that they have a Pint of mixed beer half Ale and half strong the first time, and at the other, a Pint of Ale each Man.

5th – That they be allowed cold Meat and Bread and Cheese for Supper, one Quart of Ale each Man, with One Pint of Strong Beer a Man after Supper. That they are to be allowed one hour and ½ for Supper and to drink their Beer and that no smoking or singing be allowed.

6th – That they have 10d per score for Ewes, Lambs and Tags when the whole are shorn, and 18d per score for Ewes and Tags, 14d per score for Lambs, when only a part are shorn, to have 20d per score for Shearing a Wether Flock, and in case any employer wishes to limit the number of his sheep to be shorn in one day to a less number than 40 per Man, the Company to be paid for that limited number the same as if 40 were shorn. To have 1s per hundred for winding, 3d a 100 for Black Lamb and 2s 6d per day extra for the captain and 1s for the Tar Boy.

7th – That in case of wet weather, the Men to have a Breakfast as usual, with a Quart of Ale, and wait till their employer pleases to see if there is any probability of Shearing any Sheep on that day.'

Clearly sheepshearing was thirsty work and there were plenty of fine songs sung at shearings or their associated festivities, for example this song cited by R.W. Blencowe:

'Here the rose buds in June, and the violets are blowing,
The small birds they warble from every green bough;
Here's the pink and the lily,
And the daffydowndilly,
To adorn and perfume the sweet meadows in June.
'Tis all before the plough the fat oxen go slow;
But the lads and the lasses to the sheepshearing go.'

Midsummer Eve Customs and Beliefs

Sussex legends point to Midsummer's Eve as a time of supernatural happenings and for divination. There is belief of supernatural horses on Lancing Clump on this evening, of skeletons dancing round an old oak tree on Broadwater Green near Worthing until cock-crow and of those visiting Hollingbury Camp mysteriously finding themselves back at their starting-out place in Hove. Girls carried out divination practices to ascertain the names or occupations of their husbands or the fidelity of their true loves and young men wore sprigs of the plant 'Live-long-love-long' *(Sedum telephium)* to aid their courtship. St John's Wort *(Hypericum perforatum)* was worn to keep witches away and Mugwort *(Artemisia vulgaris)* was worn to prevent the spirits of the dead from capturing anyone falling asleep on this night.

Charlotte Latham records the West Sussex tradition that:

'a stout-hearted maiden must steal out alone to the church, and sow a handful of hemp-seed, and pretend to harrow it, with anything she can drag after her, saying:

"Hemp-seed I sow, hemp-seed I grow,

If you be my true love, come after me and mow".'

Mrs Latham also mentions a tradition of maidens washing their sarks and hanging them over a chair to dry in the belief (if they maintain secrecy) that the form of their future spouse will enter the door and turn the sark. She was told of an instance when a very tall man in black did just this!

Club Walks and Sunday School Treats

Friendly Societies and Benefit Clubs and their annual summertime processions are well documented in the south of England. Members made regular small monetary contributions as insurance against sickness, unemployment, and death. The clubs' members met at regular intervals (usually in the local public house!) and in summertime, as evidenced by numerous accounts in local nineteenth century newspapers, their annual club walks were an enormous attraction. Club members arrayed in their Sunday best (the Sussex men favoured clean smocks and top hats) paraded through village or market town and its environs to the sound of the local band. A church service would follow and the day was rounded up with a celebration meal. Some nineteenth century photos of Sussex club walkers show participants carrying 6ft peeled staves. In Kent the practice was for the processions to be headed by a 'magnificent garland' in addition to the usual colours and band. An account from the *Kentish Advertiser* of June 1850 tells how the Man of Kent Benefit Society from Tovil celebrated its anniversary with a morning procession made glorious by its *'magnificent garland, colours and band'* after which all concerned attended church...and *'afterwards dined together in the club house'*. The afternoon was *'spent in the enjoyment of various rustic amusements'*. Numerous Sussex societies are documented including Petworth, Barnes Green, Chailey and Hartfield Old Club which is still in existence.

Another custom which has all but disappeared is the Sunday School Outing. Sunday Schools were started by Robert Raikes for poor children in 1780 and in the early days added general instruction to their religious teaching. Enormously popular everywhere in Britain in the nineteenth century, every church and chapel boasted a thriving Sunday School and one day each summer was set aside to give the children a 'summer treat' – an outing usually with a picnic meal and organised fun and games. Typical of accounts is this from the *Tonbridge Free Press* dated July 1900 which says that several thousand children were brought from church and chapel to the public park where a refreshment stall had been set up and *'the usual games were indulged in'* and no doubt greatly enjoyed.

Horn Fairs

The wearing of horns was an ancient symbol of power and authority in many cultures, but by the sixteenth century in England it had become associated with cuckoldry and sexual loose conduct.

The notorious Charlton Horn Fair (*'All's Fair at Horn Fair!'*), banned in 1871 but recently revived, was traditionally said to have been started under the authority of King John as recompense to the Miller of Charlton for cuckolding him – the Miller having caught the King in the act. This is a typical folk tale which has evolved to explain the goings on at the fair and has no historical basis, but various place names in the vicinity such as 'Cuckold's Point' seem to support the widespread currency of the tale (or perhaps the goings on at the fair itself). In 1700 the fair was described as *'a sanctuary for ill-manners, a protection for all rudeness, an encouragement of wickness, a revelling of young libertines, a looking glass of confusions, hurtful to all good manners and hateful to all good men.'*

The Abbot of Bermondsey was granted a charter in 1283 for an annual fair at Charlton. The 'horn' reference may connect to the bull symbol of St Luke as the fair was transferred to St Luke's Day (18th October) by the early seventeenth century. Up until the late eighteenth century, a horned procession with a King and Queen from Bishopsgate to Charlton via Rotherhithe began the fair, circling Charlton Church three times and attending a sermon.

Helena Hall, in her revisions to Parish's *Dictionary of the Sussex Dialect,* gives the following accounts of the development of the Horn Fair at the village of Ebernoe in West Sussex, which was revived in 1864 and 'cleaned up':

There is held annually a Horn Fair at Ebernoe on July 25, St James's Day, whereon they roast whole a horned sheep and whose horns are awarded as an honour to the cricketer who makes the highest score at the match played that day. The Revd. E.T. Shealey of Lurgashall tells me that in rationing days the fair was carried on, but the horned sheep was not roasted; that for two years after the War, Lord Leconfield gave a deer's horns to the man who made the highest cricket score. Many horns found in the pavilion, won by men now dead, were cleaned up and given to the winner. In 1954, after a lapse of fifteen years, the old custom was restored and a horned sheep roasted whole as before. The opposing teams are Ebernoe and Lurgashall.'

One aspect of Horn Fairs which caused offence to the puritanically minded was the dressing up of the sexes in each others' clothes. A Horn Fair song was collected by Ralph Vaughan Williams of Wotton near Dorking from Frederick Teal at the Wheatsheaf (now a gin-palace called Cromwell's) at Kingsfold, a few miles north of Horsham in West Sussex. Roy Palmer ties it to the Horn Fair at Charlton but as this was held on 18th October it seems unlikely as the song mentions 'Spring'. Some connection with Ebernoe is possible, but the late July date is still a problem. Perhaps there was another Horn Fair in our region in Spring or was the original Ebernoe Horn Fair earlier in the year?

Horn Fair Song

'As I was a-walking one morning in Spring,
So soft blew the winds and the leaves growing green;
I met a pretty damsel on a grey mare,
As she was a-riding on to Horn Fair.

I asked this pretty damsel for to let me ride.
"O no," then: "O no, my mammy would sigh:
and besides my old daddy would bid me for sure
And never let me ride on the grey mare any more.

"I can find by your talk you're for one game of play
But you will not ride me nor my grey mare today:
You will rumple my muslin and uncurl my hair
And I shouldn't be fit to be seen when I get to Horn Fair."

"O, O my pretty damsel, how can you say so,
Since it is my intention Horn Fair to go?
We will join the best of company when we do get there
With horns on our heads as fine as our hair."
There were the finest of horns as ever you did behold,
There were the finest horns as were gilded with gold;
And ride merrily, merrily, Horn Fair we did go
Like jolly brisk couples, boys, and all in a row.'

This song conveys the atmosphere and expectations of the Horn Fairs before their Victorian suppression. A fine rendering of this song by Sussex singer Bob Lewis can be found on the Veteran Tape *A Sweet Country Life* (VT 120).

Like many fairs, Black Cherry Fair, held in Chertsey on the second Saturday in July was named after the area's local produce. Now it is just another funfair.

A fair held at Chipstead, Surrey, was unexceptional except in the manner of its suppression. First recorded in 1549 during the reign of Edward VI, the annual event took place on Fair Green on St Margaret's Day, 20th July. Chipstead Church is dedicated to St Margaret and the name of nearby Mugswell is probably derived from St Mag's (or Margaret's) Well. In 1854, Shabden Manor, adjacent to the fair site, was purchased by a Mr Cattley. He, exhibiting classic 'nimby-ism', considered the fair a nuisance and similarly persuaded the Lord of the Manor, Sir W. George Hylton-Joliffe. Joliffe, in turn, instructed his steward to call in the Reigate Police who turned away the fairgoers as they arrived on the green. The operation was smooth and efficient, leaving the gentry delighted and the lower orders disgruntled if partly mollified by Cattley's promise to inaugurate a cricket match to replace the fair. A letter of Pecksniffian magnitude dated 21st July 1854 from steward Thomas Hart to his employer declared the writer *'satisfied that a great moral good has been effected'*. This is an unfortunate example of a Victorian tendency to tamper with working class customs under the guise of moral supremacy.

Swan Upping c,1990   (Doc Rowe Collection)

Derby Day

In 1779 the Earl of Derby held a house-party at 'The Oaks', a converted inn near Woodmansterne. Derby himself and a group of sporting friends, in their cups, declared the need for a horse-race without the then-customary but exhausting preliminary heats. Thus was born the Oaks, named after the house, originally for 3-year old fillies and colts but now solely for fillies. The following year, 1780, gave birth to the Derby; it is said that the toss of a coin between Lord Derby and Sir Charles Bunbury decided the race's name but there is no evidence for this. A good story though: what would have become of a race called the Bunbury? In fact, Bunbury is a far more important figure than Derby in the history of horse-racing. Regarded as Perpetual President of the Jockey Club, his memory survives at Newmarket, the Bunbury Mile, and his horse Diomed was the first Derby Winner.

The race was originally run on Thursdays but by the late 1830s the first Wednesday in June was Derby Day, as it remained until 1994. Mammon then raised his head in the guise of international television and the race will be run on Saturdays from 1995. From the start Epsom Downs became the focus for an unofficial public holiday. Itinerant musicians, hawkers and fairground folk came to the course; race-goers mingled with the great congress of gipsies from all over the British Isles. Colourful crowds walked to Epsom from Coulsdon, Dorking, Horley and Reigate. Happily, if less colourful, those from Reigate still do.

Swan Upping on the Thames: 'nicking' (marking) the birds.   (Sir Benjamin Stone)

Swan Upping on the Thames: examining the old birds.   (Sir Benjamin Stone)

At 7am on Derby Day some Reigate pubs open their doors to serve breakfast and drinks; it would be impolitic to name them as the opening is unofficial! There the walkers congregate, having their first drinks of a long day and then set off in twos, threes or larger groups to cover the seven miles to Epsom Downs. The walk is not organised: it just happens. The only rule is that no pub on the cross-country route should be passed without sampling its wares. Many of the walkers take part simply for the joy of being there, not through any interest in racing. Indeed, the talk is rarely of horses, rather of previous walks and the one to come. Often the alcohol takes its toll, with walkers arriving on course too late for the race and return journeys made by public transport. Hardier walkers, though, complete their day by returning on foot, or sometimes hands-and-knees, to their starting-points.

The Derby Day revellers of Reigate should thank Tony Nash, ex-landlord of a local pub, and the late John Priestman, who revived the Derby Walk as a mass event in the early 1970s.

Little Edith's Treat

A curious custom takes place at Piddinghoe, on the banks of the Ouse near Newhaven, on 19th July, known as 'Little Edith's Treat'. When Edith Croft died in 1868 aged three months, her grandmother made an endowment of £100 to be expended on the baby's birthday. This is celebrated by a church service followed by children's races and tea.

Swan-Upping

Swans belong to the monarch of the day except for a certain number of Thames birds which have since the 1470s been the property of the London Guilds of Vintners and Dyers, sole survivors of various bodies once entitled to 'swan-rights' on the Thames. Since Elizabeth I's reign these two companies of Vintners and Dyers have organised an annual 'Swan Voyage' along the Thames from Monday to Thursday in the third full week of July, when the cygnets are about two months old. The swans are removed from the water, 'upped', and the adults checked by marked beaks, denoting the Company birds, and unmarked beaks, the royal variety. Cygnets attached to each swan are marked or left alone according to their parentage, while their wings are clipped to prevent them straying too far from the Thames. Vintners' swans have their beaks nicked twice – hence the pub name, 'The Swan with Two Necks' – and Dyers' swans once.

During the seventeenth and eighteenth centuries the Vintners and Dyers owned magnificent state barges, sadly no more, but the Swan-Upping ceremony is still a colourful sight. Six rowing-boats set out from Sunbury-on-Thames (originally from the City of London), two each belonging to the Crown, the Vintners Company and the Dyers Company and all propelled by men wearing red jerseys. The Queen's Swanherd, resplendent in royal livery, travels in one boat flying the royal banner from the prow and another flag depicting a swan aft. One of the Vintners' boats carries their Swan Marker, in green livery, while in another boat the Dyers' Swan Marker is similarly clad but in blue. The Companies' boats each fly a single flag

Swan Upping, c1990   (Doc Rowe Collection)

bearing the Company Arms and a picture of a swan. The three teams of 'uppers' work together to herd the birds and it can be both difficult and dangerous to trap an angry swan. When the upping is completed each year the Companies hold a Swan Banquet.

Day of Syn

Every second year (even years) at the end of August a 'Day of Syn Festival' is held at Dymchurch on Romney Marsh to commemorate Russell Thorndike's fictional, yet archetypal and immensely influential, smuggler, Doctor Syn. Mock battles are held between smugglers and preventive-men and soldiers and a mounted Doctor Syn himself appears in his favourite guise as 'The Scarecrow'. This event is well organised and publicised and great fun and details can be obtained of future events from Shepway District Council.

The Gibson Legacy

St Nicholas's churchyard in Sutton boasts a magnificent tomb containing this inscription:

> *'Within this tomb lyes the Remains of*
> *James Gibson Esqr and family*
> *Late Merchant and Citizen of London*
> *To whose memory this tomb was erected*
> *1777'*

A plaque outside the tomb informs the reader that:

'This Mausoleun built in 1777, is the family tomb of the London wine merchant, James Gibson (c1706-1776), Master of the Iron-Mongers' Company. In accordance with the will of the last of the Gibson family, Miss Mary Gibson (c1730-1793), the tomb is the subject of an annual inspection on August 12th.'

Ambrose Bierce described a mausoleum as *'the ultimate folly of the rich and famous'*. The Gibson family of Sutton were not especially famous, but bequests in James Gibson's will suggest that his capital stood at £20,000, a considerable amount for the late 1700s. James was a distiller and brandy-merchant, an urbane man, and, as the plaque states, it was not he but his eccentric daughter Mary who left instructions that the family vault was to be opened for inspection on 12th August each year. Why that date was chosen is not clear for she died on 10th October 1793. Arthur Mee, in 1938, suggested that Mary's request was designed to deter grave-robbers from stealing bodies from the vault for medical experimentation.

Mary Gibson presented the Governors of Christ's Hospital School, then in the City of London, with the responsibility for ensuring that the rector and churchwardens of St Nicholas' Church carried out her wishes. She left money to those who performed the ceremony of inspection and to the Hospital itself. Parochial charities took over in 1862 but, until then, gifts of money and clothing were given to the poor of Sutton Parish. Should Christ's Hospital fail in its duties, Miss Gibson decreed, then the responsibilities should be transferred to the Foundling Hospital, an eventuality that never arose.

The ceremony was first performed in 1794, the year after Mary's death, and continued to attract considerable public interest, despite the church being rebuilt in 1863, until1989. Then the Reverend David Hazlehurst, who kindly supplied most of this information, called a halt. He points out that the Gibson family had never intended the opening and inspecting of their tomb to become 'a public spectacle' and that the money to assist the poor had greatly diminished. He also believes that what may be regarded as a 'queer and irrelevant' practice shows scant respect for the Gibson remains. However, the churchwardens still carry out a private inspection every 12th August to fulfil the terms of the bequest. It may be that Mary Gibson herself still takes an interest, too, as her ghost is said to emerge occasionally from the urn surmounting her mausoleum.

Ken Thompson at his Faversham Hop Farm, 1950s. (Glenn Miller)

Hoppers huts, Museum of Kent Life at Cobtree. (Geoff Doel)

Chapter Eight
HARVEST
Hopping and Harvest Home

The completion of the gathering in of the harvest had highly significant practical and symbolic meaning for the farming communities of the three counties. Mild climate and fertile soil gained Kent the epithet 'The Garden of England' and it was famed for its cherries, apples and market gardens. It was additionally once Britain's chief hop-growing district and its landscape is still made distinctive by the large number of oast houses or drying kilns with their conical roofs. Hops are usually ready for harvesting towards the end of August and it was then that the hop-pickers – men, women and children – arrived in the fields of Kent in their thousands, many making hop-picking the occasion for their annual holiday. Until the late 1950s fields full of 6-metre poles carrying networks of strong wire which supported the growing hop, men on stilts walking up and down the rows, and the hop-pickers huts, often of corregated iron, were a common sight. Nowadays in the few remaining hop fields the vines are pulled from the wires and carried by tractor to a machine which strips and separates hop cones and leaves and delivers the fruit into sacks.

In Kent, the last days of hopping were often a time of harvest celebration. Many farms had a tea-party for the hoppers' children (who had often formed an unofficial part of the workforce) followed by a hopping supper for the adult workers in the evening. The venue for this was traditionally the oast house in which the hops had been dried and packed. On some large farms there was an election of a King and Queen of the Hops, followed by a considerable amount of drinking, and a dance to round off the day. This was also the day on which the pickers wore decorated hats using dog daises, convolvulus, tulips, cornflowers and the hop itself. Whitbreads Farm, one of the biggest employers of pickers from the East End of London, from 1935 onwards concluded the harvest with open air dancing and the election of a Hop Queen. The new Queen, crowned and robed in a velvet cloak, was drawn in procession in a hop cart by one of the famous Whitbread shire horses. One old custom was the burning in effigy of someone disliked in the hop-garden – the bin man and measurer the likeliest candidates. However, the oldest custom (commented on by George Orwell when picking in 1931) was the throwing of young girls and men into the bin *for devilment and good luck*. They came to no harm for hop 'bins' are cradles of sacking on wooden supports and they would have been full of hops.

Sussex once had many hop gardens, but wheat was the most important cereal grown in our three counties, with some oats, barley and rye. Today modern machinery ensures swift harvesting with a minimal workforce, but the harvesting of these cereals once involved whole communities.

Lucy Baldwin and Arthur Ridsdale describe the picturesque if back-breaking harvesting of wheat in Rottingdean in the 1880s and the celebrations that followed:

'...The harvest was cut with a reaping hook or sickle and then the swap hook. The straw was cut close to the ground. This sort of work was often given to men out of work or to tramps. They slept in hovels and barns whilst the harvest time lasted. After being cut by hand the bands were united together by two wisps of straw tied close to the ears by a particular knot and were then stacked in shocks or stooks. Occasionally a rabbit or two was found in the last part of the uncut corn and became 'perks' for those who caught them. After the cutting of the corn there came a small company of gleaners, children and adults, mostly women, to gather up the ears that were left. The village children's summer holidays always coincided with the harvest time, and it was a pretty sight, the elderly women wearing sun bonnets, they were worn then by all women over a certain age, as well as by some of the little girls. They used to do their gleaning in rows, the women first and the children behind, and the coloured sun bonnets were very attractive bobbing up and down.

'When all the harvest was finished we had the harvest supper and harvest beer. The last load was carried in a large farm waggon with flags flying, many children and men sitting on top of the last load, while the carter led the horses. Healths were drunk in glorious beer, and boys and men sang in chorus the following refrain:

"We plough, we sow, we reap, we mow,
We've carried our last load and ain't other (over) throwed!
Hip, hip, hurrah etc."

'They pulled up at each public house and each private residence in turn as they went the round of the village.'

In all three counties the last sheaf was often made into a corn dolly to symbolise the spirit of the corn and a harvest supper held by the farmer for his workfolk on a nearby Saturday. Tony Wales describes the harvest home of 1863 at West Hoathly in Sussex:

'The day began at 8am with the church bells ringing. The main street was decorated with flags and greenery, and at 1.30pm a service was held in the church. This was followed by a procession led by the village band; farmers had provided waggons and there were such things in the parade as a huge loaf of bread carried on a wooden tray. The landowners had contributed two shillings each to contribute to the feast, which was held in a marquee in Cross Field. The meal included quantities of beef, potatoes, suet pudding, plum cake, and gingerbread. The wives and children had a separate tent, in which they had a lighter meal of tea and cakes. Afterwards, those who were in a fit state were invited to take part in sports, with various prizes.'

The following Harvest Home song was collected from the late Charlie Heasman of Reigate in the early 1970s:

Opposite: Gipsy hop-pickers, turn of the century.

'O the Summer's in its prime and the flowers are all in bloom
And the small birds are singing all around;
O the dew is on the grass and it's Harvest time at last
But we've time for another round, my boys,
    We've time for another round.

Leave the women to their tasks while we do take our flasks
And drink to the year's bonny crop;
Before we start to mow to the alehouse we will go
For we've time for another drop, my boys,
    We've time for another drop.

Leave the Master while we may, now we've time enough for play,
Though tomorrow there'll be no rest for man;
Then the Harvest will begin and the corn will fill the bin
But we've time for another can, my boys,
    We've time for another can.

So come all you countrymen and fill the jug again,
Let's drink a toast to each jovial soul
Who likes his beer each day and merrily will say:
"We've time for another bowl, my boys,
    We've time for another bowl."'

Michaelmas

Few customs are as bizarre as that of Surrey's 'Crack Nut Sunday' which had its demise in the late eighteenth century. In Kingston Parish Church on the Sunday prior to Michaelmas Day (September 29th) the entire congregation were permitted to indulge in the cracking and eating of nuts during the service. One explanation is that this noisy practice may have been transferred from an annual civic feast in which bailiffs and other members of the Corporation were elected. Ultimately known as 'Crack Nut Sunday', the day was eventually silenced when the noise became too deafening for the preacher's sermon to be heard!

BIBLIOGRAPHY

General

J. Brand *Observations on the Popular Antiquities of Great Britain* (London 1848-9)

Geoffrey Chaucer *The Parliament of Fowls* in *Collected Works of Chaucer* ed F. Robinson (Oxford 1970)

Margaret Gascoigne *Discovering English Customs and Traditions* (Shire 1969)

Christina Hole *A Dictionary of British Folk Customs* (Hutchinson 1976)

David Holloway *Derby Day* (Michael Joseph 1975)

Roy Judge *The Jack in the Green: A May Day Custom* (Cambridge: D.S. Brewer 1979)

Roy Judge *May Day in England – An Introductory Bibliography* (EFDSS 1988)

Charles Kightly *The Customs and Ceremonies of Britain* (Thames & Hudson 1986)

Bob Pegg *Rites & Riots* (Blandford 1981)

Cecil Sharp, Herbert Macilwaine & George Butterworth *The Morris Book* (2nd edition Novello 1912)

Brian Shuel *The National Trust Guide to Traditional Customs of Britain* (Webb & Bower 1985)

Jacqueline Simpson *British Dragons* (Batsford 1980)

Arthur Taylor *The Guinness Book of Traditional Pub Games* (Guinness 1992)

David Wiles *The Early Plays of Robin Hood,* (Cambridge Brewer 1981)

Kent

Biddenden Local History Society *The Story of Biddenden* (Biddenden Local History Society, 1980)

William Bray (ed) *The Diary and Correspondence of John Evelyn* (Henry Colburn, 1854)

Gentleman's Magazine (1779)

Alan Glencross *The Buildings of Greenwich* (London Borough of Greenwich Local History Library)

Jack Hamilton (ed) (EFDSS) *Folk in Kent* series of magazines.

Edward Hasted *History and Topographical Survey of Kent* (Canterbury 1798)

Gilbert Hoole *A Tonbridge Miscellany*

Don Minifie *May Day at Whitstable (English Dance & Song* EFDSS Spring 1978)

W.D. Parish & W.F. Shaw *A New Dictionary of Kent Dialect* augmented by Alan Major (Meresborough 1981)

ed Latham & Mathews *The Diary of Samuel Pepys* (Bell & Sons 1970)

Taylor *Jack-a-Lent* (1630)

Thomas Trowsdale *Garland Day in West Kent* (The Antiquary, June 1880)

Richard Harman (ed) *Countryside Mood* (Blandford Press undated)
Newspapers: *The Tonbridge Free Press*
Periodicals: the *Quarterly Association of Men of Kent and Kentish Men* (no. 158, April 1963)

Surrey

Matthew Alexander *Tales of Old Surrey* (Countryside Books 1985)
Matthew Alexander *More Surrey Tales* (Countryside Books 1986)
George Clinch & S.W. Kershaw (eds) *Bygone Surrey* (Simpkins, Marshall Hamilton, Kent & Co. 1895)
Lewis G. Fry (ed) *Oxted, Limpsfield & Neighbourhood* (no publisher or date)
Arthur B. Hayward & Stanley Hazell (eds) *A History of Lingfield* (Courier 1933)
Margaret K. Kohler (ed) *Memories of Old Dorking* (Kohler & Coombes 1977)
Edward Lovett *Folklore & Legend of the Surrey Hills & of the Sussex Downs & Forests* (Caterham Valley 1928, Folklore Society Reprint 1991)
F.E. Manning *Surrey Past & Present* (Surrey County Council 1971)
Arthur Mee *Surrey* (Hodder & Stoughton 1938)
Eric Parker *Highways & Byways in Surrey* (Macmillan 1908)
Eric Parker *Surrey* (Robert Hale 1947)
Charles E. Pringle *A History of Chipstead* (Chipstead Valley Preservation Society 1984)
G.R. Rolston *Haslemere* (Phillimore 1978)
Charles Rose *Recollections of Old Dorking* (West Surrey Times 1878)
June Sampson *The Story of Kingston* (Michael Lancet 1972)
Surrey Federation of Women's Institutes (compilers) *Surrey Within Living Memory* (Countryside Books & Surrey WI 1992)
E.W. Swanton & P. Woods *Bygone Haslemere* (West, Newman & Co 1914)
Dorothy Tutt *Thomas Kelly* (Local History Records vol. XI 1972: The Bourne Society for Caterham and Warlingham, Coulsdon and Purley)
Newspapers: *The County Chronicle & Weekly Advertiser; The Surrey Advertiser & County Times; The Surrey Mirror*
Periodicals: The Bourne Society Local History Records (Reigate); *Surrey History; The Wotton Quarterly*
The E.L. Sellick Collection, Dorking Museum

Sussex

Anon *The Brighton Custumal* (ms 1580)
Lucy Baldwin & Arthur Ridsale *Annals of Old Rottingdean* (Sussex Notes & Queries 1933)
R.W. Blencowe *South Down Shepherds and Their Songs at Sheepshearing* (Sussex Archaeological Collections 1849)
Henry Burstow *Reminiscences of Horsham* (1911)
Lilian Candlin *Memories of Old Sussex* (Countryside Books 1987)
Bob Copper *A Song For Every Season* (Heinemann 1971)

Charlotte Latham *West Sussex Superstitions* (Folk-lore Record, vol. 1 1878)

Keith Leech *The Hastings Jack in the Green* (South East Arts)

Rev. W.D. Parish *A Dictionary of Sussex Dialect* (Farncombe 1875; expanded by Helena Hall (Gardners 1981)

Sam McCarthy *Pop Maynard – Lord of the Ring (English Dance & Song* EFDSS, Spring 1982)

Frederick Sawyer *Sussex Folklore and Customs Connected With the Seasons* (Sussex Archaeological Collection 1883)

Jacqueline Simpson *The Folklore of Sussex* (Batsford 1973)

Ken Stubbs *The Life and Songs of George Maynard* (EFDSS 1963)

Sussex Notes & Queries *Sheep Sheares' Customs* (vol. II pp 24/5)

Tony Wales *Sussex Customs, Curiosities & County Lore* (Ensign 1990)

Tony Wales *A Sussex Garland* (Countryside Books 1979)

Tony Wales *We Wunt be Druv – songs & stories from Sussex* (Galliard: EFDSS 1976)

ACKNOWLEDGEMENTS

To **Matthew Alexander,** Curator of Guildford Museum, for extensive details of the Tyting Dancing and for other information.

To **Gladys Arlett & Brian Hodges,** the Curators of the excellent Dorking Museum, for assistance with records and photographs of the Dorking Shrovetide Football and John Evelyn's Diary.

To **Alan Austen** for information on early references to Morris Dancing and on the Kent revival team to which he belongs, Mr Jorrocks.

To **Phil Burkin** for information and photographs of Hartley Morris.

To **Olive Doel** for information on Good Friday skipping.

To **Tony Foxworthy, Alan Austen & Keith Leech** for information and interesting discussions on Jacks-in-the-Green, (and to Tony for the photo of the Jack-in-the-Green at Lambeth).

To **George Fry** of Tonbridge School & The Tonbridge Mummers & **Gilbert Hoole** Tonbridge author & historian for information on Skinners Day and Green Boughs at Tonbridge School.

To **Tony Gowan** of Reigate Adult Education Service and the Cowden Mummers, for the taped conversation with his aunt about Shrovetide Football in Dorking, for the unstinting use of his vast library of Surrey history and for photographs.

To **Florence Grey** for information on May Day at Shoreham, Sussex.

To **The Reverend David Hazelhurst** of St Nicholas' Church, Sutton, for copious notes on the Gibson Legacy.

To **Sam McCarthy Fox,** Secretary to the British Marbles Board of Control, for details of the Tinsley Green Marbles Championship.

To **Mr R. Merrifield** for his photo on Good Friday skipping at Brighton.

To **Doc Rowe** for his photographs of Swan-Upping and the Chanctonbury Morris Men and years of fruitful discussion.

To **Archie Turnbull** for his photo of the Tonbridge Mummers.

To **Dorothy Tutt** for information on the Kelly Bequest.

To **Tony Wales,** whose books on Sussex traditions have been a great inspiration, and for his permission to use his photos of May Garlands and Beating the Bounds at Hastings.

To **David Watts,** of Elsie's Band, for his memories and photographs of the Climping Dragon ceremony.

To **David Andrews, Mary & Mick Blackie, Philip Case, Bob Davies, Kerensa Deane, Colin Gates, Richard Larque, Venetia Newall, Dick Richardson** and **Jim Ward,** for their general help and comments.

To the staff of Public Libraries at Canterbury, Chichester, Croydon, Dorking, Guildford, Maidstone, Redhill, Reigate, Sutton, Tonbridge & Tunbridge Wells; Museums at Chichester, Dorking, Guildford, Kingston and Maidstone and the Sussex Archaeological Society.